THE CRUMB ROAD

Maitreyabandhu was born Ian Johnson in Warwickshire in 1961. He initially trained as a nurse at the Walsgrave Hospital, Coventry, then went on to study fine art at Goldsmiths College, London.

He started attending classes at the London Buddhist Centre (LBC) in 1986, and moved into a residential spiritual community above the LBC in 1987. He was ordained into the Triratna Buddhist Order in 1990 and given the name Maitreyabandhu. Since then he has lived and worked at the LBC, teaching Buddhism and meditation. He has written two books on Buddhism, *Thicker than Blood: Friendship on the Buddhist Path* (2001) and *Life with Full Attention: a Practical Course in Mindfulness* (2009) both with Windhorse Publications. His forthcoming book *The Journey and the Guide*, also with Windhorse, is due in 2014. In 2010 he founded Poetry East, a new poetry venue exploring the relationship between spiritual life and poetry, and attracting many of the UK's foremost poets. He has also published articles in *Poetry Review, Poem, Magma, Agenda, Assent* and *In Their Own Words: Contemporary Poets on their Poetry* (Salt, 2012).

Maitreyabandhu has won the Keats-Shelley Prize, the Basil Bunting Award, the Geoffrey Dearmer Prize, and the Ledbury Festival Poetry Competition. His first pamphlet *The Bond* won the Poetry Business Book and Pamphlet Competition (2010) and was shortlisted for the Michael Marks Award. *Vita Brevis*, his second pamphlet, winner of the Iota Shots Award and a Poetry Book Society Pamphlet Choice, was published by Templar in 2013. His first book-length collection, *The Crumb Road*, is published by Bloodaxe in 2013 and is a Poetry Book Society Recommendation.

MAITREYABANDHU

THE CRUMB ROAD

BLOODAXE BOOKS

ISBN: 978 1 85224 974 8

First published 2013 by
Bloodaxe Books Ltd,
Highgreen,
Tarset,
Northumberland NE48 1RP.

www.bloodaxebooks.com
For further information about Bloodaxe titles
please visit our website or write to
the above address for a catalogue.

Supported by
**ARTS COUNCIL
ENGLAND**

For Mimi Khalvati

Cover design: Neil Astley & Pamela Robertson-Pearce.

Printed in Great Britain by
Bell & Bain Limited, Glasgow, Scotland.

This

There's no law against my listening
to this thrush behind the barn,
the song so loud it echoes like a bell,
then it's further off beyond the lawn.
Whatever else there is, there's this as well.

There's no law against this singing –
nesting I suppose – up in the silver birch,
even though we build a common hell,
have done, and will make it worse.
Whatever else there is, there's this as well.

ACKNOWLEDGEMENTS

Some of these poems, or earlier versions of them, were published in *Agenda, Assent, The Guardian, The Interpreter's House, Iota, The Keats-Shelley Review, Magma, The New Writer, Poetry Review, The North, Oxford Poetry, Prole, The Rialto, Shearsman, Smiths Knoll, Stand, The Warwick Review* and *Urthona*.

'Visitation' won the Manchester Cathedral International Religious Poetry Competition (2007) and the Geoffrey Dearmer Prize (2009). 'The Small Boy and the Mouse' won the Keats-Shelley Prize (2009). 'The Coat Cupboard' won the Basil Bunting Award (2009). 'The Cutting' won the Ledbury Festival Poetry Competition (2010). 'Uchida from the Choir Stalls' was runner-up in the Nottingham Open (2009) and was selected for *The Best British Poetry 2011* (Salt Publishing).

The Crumb Road contains poems from *Bird Thoughts*, which won the New Writer Prose and Poetry Competition (2009); *The Bond*, which won the Poetry Business Book and Pamphlet Competition (2010) and was shortlisted for the Michael Marks Award (2012); and *Vita Brevis*, which won the Iota Shots Award (2012) and is a PBS Pamphlet Choice. The poem 'Letters on Cézanne' contains material from Rilke's letters (see *Letters on Cézanne* edited by Clara Rilke).

I'd like to thank Fiona Sampson, Carol Rumens, Peter Sansom, David Constantine and Jane Draycott for their help and encouragement. I am especially grateful to Vishvantara Julia Lewis and Mimi Khalvati, without whose help this collection would not have been possible. And I am greatly indebted to the Jerwood/Arvon and Escalator mentoring schemes, and to the Arts Council England for their generous support.

CONTENTS

III STEPHEN

I.

Uchida from the Choir Stalls

Before she plays, a man adjusts the microphones
on their tall strategic stands – one above her stool
where soon she'll sit in bottle-green transparency,
another high above the strings. And when applause
breaks out, and she strides to take her place,
we wait while she sits at the piano, hands suspended
till the coughing stops. Music filters down the snaking
lengths of flex to a van outside, where a man
sits drinking coffee in front of luminous dials –
streetlights blinking, the pavement's crush of youth.

And where it takes me, the violas lifting something
that might have once been sad, is to a double garage
that had been my father's shed, tools suspended
in long Dutch shadows, an atmosphere of industry
and wood-dust. He moves about in his oily coat
and green wool hat, sharpening a chisel, chamfering
an edge, his pockets full of tissues where we'd later
find the keys. He oils a cross-peen hammer and hangs it
in a bag, along with all the other tools from car boot sales
and farms: broken things that once sat quietly in his palm.

There's a place in Poland, or so I'm told, where all
the men are carpenters and all the houses wood.
Apple trees crowd around their doors, paths lead to pines
and hewn titanic oaks. All the men have wolf-cub eyes
and make pencil calculations on their walls. Their speech
is large and deliberate like the writing desks they build;
even their breakfast bowls are teak, and all their spoons
and knives. Leaf-light shines in at their rooms, catching
walnut beds and jugs. At night they hum a Polish tune:
it is long and very sad, though no one knows the words.

Burial

My father was digging below the lilac trees
when his spade broke the crown of a buried skull.

The stench, he told me, clambered through his chest,
then through his head, like a shirking ghost.

He was soon unearthing bones. He brought
the second skull indoors with clods of earth

still hanging from its jowl and stood it on
the *Stratford Herald* while my mother protested,

men gathered from the yard and the dog
hid under the table. But that isn't right,

I've made it up or rather I've mistaken
my father's story for the thing itself:

the smell, the wormy skull, the policeman
tall, bright-buttoned, standing by the Aga.

The Coat Cupboard

Once you close the door, once you're in, you're small
like you've shrunk – no window, no view of sycamores,
cattle or an aqueduct – a stand-alone place
big enough for one. The walls and the back of the door
are lined with coats, two or three deep, hanging
on high brass hooks: gabardines, parkas, macks –
the smart black coat your father never liked, the knitted
afternoon jacket that might've been your aunt's
and shoes unevenly stacked so that you almost stumble
and twist your ankle on the heel of a brogue.
You don't push your way through to discover a landscape
where beavers can talk; you're not reunited with your lover
coming around the headland in a ship – your face
is pressed against lambswool and the smell of camphor,
ink and dogs. Your fingers, which have become
unaccountably small and white, ferret in the pockets
of a waxed raincoat, among coins and balled-up
silver paper, folded receipts and pencil shavings.
And there are shadows between the coats, long scarves
of shadow that disappear when you touch them
like crows flying up from a field. You find a set of keys
without their brightness or warmth of handling –
leather keyring almost worn through at the hoop,
the aluminium badge with a profile of a swan – and a lipstick
your grandma must have used, the 50s pink
when you wind it out, still shaped to the curve of her lip.

Potato

The teacher was talking at the front; she said
Keep going and *Very good* and now and then
a girl would pass wearing a smile of triumph.
My jumper was another hand-me-down –
Another Johnson boy? the headmaster said
when I had to say my name, the name
my mother told me wouldn't shorten, written
above the peg. Now it was my turn:
the boy in front had read about a dog
and got it right, so I was ushered forward.

My ears were hot. *Read from here* she said.
I started well enough (they were easy words)
but soon I saw a big one coming up
and hoped she'd say to stop before I got there.
Each little word got harder as the big word
came along. I tripped. The word got stuck.
I couldn't spit it out. *Go on* she said.
The room smelt of biro ink and satchels.
I could see my mother's arms; they were freckled
but the freckles kept on getting in the way.

What does it begin with? She pointed
at the word. Her voice was coming from
the snowy picture pinned up on the wall.
Puh I managed *Puh...* The teacher's desk
had ink stains like the lakes I'd heard about
and someone had gouged a river and a name.
You'll stand in front of class until you say it!
said the snow with its seven pointed stars.
The room was bright and far away; beyond
the frosted window a black dog chased its tail.

The Medium

When my best friend's mother died, he went
with his sister to see a Medium who talked
of Namaste Namaste and Sell the House –
husband reunited with wife and everything
reconciled and Joy, my friend said, Joy!

Which brought to mind the man from the drycleaner's
when Nana died, who turned up at the yard
and said, 'Your mother keeps on coming through.
Can you sit with us tonight?' My mother
struggled with saying No without offence.

But when he tapped the office glass, Ajax
must have barked, then slunk under the desk
and sighed as dogs will do before lying down
and watching from the dark where I see
my mother as a child, buttoned up

against the snowy streets of Shirley, cycling
with her brother behind her mother's bike
that Christmas Eve during the war – the creak
and tick of bikes, all the signposts gone,
Nana looking her best and wearing lipstick.

After that my mother wouldn't speak
or said that it was nothing. But what I remember
was the blouse she wore and often wore
those days: polycotton with thin brown lines
like cycle tracks and *ok ok ok* in the margin.

Bottle Digging

I wasn't as good at digging as my dad.
He could dig a hole, say, six-feet deep –
spading out one side then turning round
and spading out the other. He'd use a fork
to ferret in the sides, then loosen up
the ground under his boots, careful not
to break whatever might be buried – a cod
if he was lucky, with a marble stoppered
in the top, but more likely a Derby beer
or a broken toothpaste lid. He'd rub them
with his glove, read the letters embossed
on the side, then chuck them up the top
ready to bring home in a cardboard box.
And once he dug so deep, the other diggers
had to pull him up so he could eat his lunch.

I didn't have the heart much less the strength.
I'd root around not hoping to find much –
HP Sauce and broken china – then one day
out at Snitterfield or Warwick in rough ground
well dug-over, with potholes in between
the tall and dusty nettles – it was summer
and every spade-full reeked of rusty tin –
I found a cottage ink, pale blue or rather
bluish-green, with bubbles in the glass:
a little thing, and yes, shaped like a cottage
with windows at the front, a wonky door
and doorstep, markings where slates would be
and a chimney sharpened at the top.

I gave the house a little shake to empty
out the soil, then went to show my dad,
who was digging near the road – a pint
of milk ready propped up in the shade.
A man came over to look at what I'd found,

then offered me a cod and two brown beers
in fair exchange. Dad was saying nothing.
I walked over with the man to where his van
was parked. I thought I'd done a deal, although
it hurt like stones to hand the cottage over.
He called me Ian, then slapped my shoulder hard.

Dad had put the tools inside the boot
when I got back. We drove in silence home.
And after that he made it known to anyone
who'd listen that I'd been duped by a collector
who would even stoop to cheat a kid.
And I'm still ashamed of what I did.

The Newt

I opened an art school in the conservatory
of number 32. Everyone was given names –
Secretary to the Pencil Committee,
Rubber Monitor. A boy with eczema

drew a train; someone coloured in a flower.
The Christmas turkey was hanging in the corner
with its throat slit and blood
dripping from its neck into a metal basin.

My brothers called it the Rear Gunner:
they'd turned the old green lorry into a Lancaster
and bounce-bombed the dams –
unless that was later when we kept chickens

in the greenhouse next to the water butt
where I found a spotted newt?
Two cockerels, dreadful things,
fought to the death among the cauliflowers.

Copper Wire

My brothers ran along ahead, my sister
talked and swung a bucketful of shells.
Rabbit paths and sheep paths led away
in a delta of directions between heather
and scattered rocks; some to where the updraft
from the shore made us hug our coats
and some to stiles and sheltered farms and hedges.
My father looked for barren ground, a dump
with weird bits of metal sticking up
or some grey ash. My mother would be hoping
for a sunset, though it often clouded over
just before the end. We'd sit together
on the slippery grass and watch the sky turn grey,
then wander back to where we'd parked the car.
My father would be pulling something lively
from the ground, a struggling silhouette.
We'd lose him in the cry of famished gulls.
Eventually the boys would run and get him –
he'd catch us up and say *Copper wire!*
then smile and rub the crumbling coating off
until it shone like fraying hoops of gold.

Makings

You made an owl in woodwork from a piece
of apple-wood your father found – a block
you took to school and worked from period bell
to bell, unable to carve the bony claws
but relishing the fall-away of breast,
the feather marks and wild, dartboard eyes.
You rubbed beeswax into its folded wings,
then put it on the mantelpiece and liked it
standing among the Christmas cards and tinsel.
It was weeks or even months before the dog,
a young alsatian you took out after school,
pulled it down and chewed away the face.

You made a model out of chicken wire
and the *Daily Mail*. You made a man walking
his dog across the fields. You gave the man
a coat with three white buttons. But the dog
was beyond you and the man was never right.
You knew it all along. He was out of proportion,
his knees set too high up, his legs too long.
His face, the thumb-pressed hollows of his eyes,
expressed nothing. You gave him painted shoes,
a stick to hold, then stood him on a shelf.
No one said anything about the man
or drew attention to him in any way.

This was the time of motocross: your brothers
going to ride at Church Lench or Meon Hill
and you staying at home to paint a picture
of your father from a photo of him
standing by the stove and turning round.
Everything was brown – his V-neck jersey,
patterned tie, the kitchen cupboards behind him.
The dog was fast asleep under the table
where you worked. You were altering
the jaw-line, very slightly, with the tip
of a filbert brush, when there he was!
your father, looking up at you and smiling.

Hammers

No one wanted the tools my father bought
at car boot sales and garage sales and farms:
claw hammer, tack hammer, the ornate
toffee hammer with a tiny pickaxe head.
Sometimes the handles had to be repaired –
he'd chisel where the rot was worst, blowing
out the dust, then glue a piece of ash
and clamp it in. He'd cut a wedge of brass
to make the shaft fit tighter to the head,
then he'd work away with wire wool and turps.
Each hammer had to marinade for weeks
in linseed oil wrapped up in plastic bags.
They'd hang around the shed like dusty trophies
until he'd take one down and show us all
the glowing afterlife of wood. He'd close
his hand around them just to feel the smoothness
running through his palm, and when he died
we left them hanging in their bags. None of us
could face the task of clearing out the shed.

The Chest of Drawers

I ran along the lilac path to go and see her
in the darkened room where, dressed in black,
she sat with two alsatians at her feet.
She showed me how to dust between the rungs
of a wooden chair – you held the duster
at either end, then pulled one end then the other.
She taught me to draw a swan without lifting
the crayon off my pad, a triple loop
that finished with the head and beak. And once
I coloured in a goose, bright yellow, without going
over the lines; she was so pleased she told
my mother I was sure to be all right.

I'd follow my mother round the house and watch her
dust and shine; she'd let me hold the polish tin
while she ironed my older brothers' shirts
or hoovered up the lounge. She'd roll our socks
inside each other and press them into drawers.
I'd watch her make the beds. She'd tuck the sheets
and blankets in so tight, you had to wriggle
when you got in to make a proper space!
I'd ask her what to dream about; she'd say
'The dog' or 'Sailing out to sea' – anything
to keep away the nightmares I would have
about a man locked inside an iron mask.

Archaeology

Two white tents at the end of Irelands Lane
edged the dig where carefully-written signs
– potash, clinker, brick-and-tile and clay –
marked the multi-layered drift of time.

Trestle tables were covered with bone pieces
and metal stakes had been pushed into the ground
like how my father ordered his potatoes.
I trowelled between the cobblestones I found

at such-a-depth. The mud came up in curlicues.
The rank profusion of nettles and cuckoo spit
made me think the dead still fed the earth.

I was sleeping in the bunk above my sister.
We'd argue about whose side the light was on,
then I'd tell her about Tutankhamun's curse.

Shark Fishing

We hired a boat and a Cornish fisherman,
then stepped gingerly on board, my mother
going first – the skipper reaching out
as she stepped across the gap – my brothers
(each a year or so apart), my sister

small and smiling, and last of all my father
enquiring about the weather or the tides.
We pushed off from the jetty while our captain
pulled the heavy coils of rope that splashed us
when they came aboard. The day was fine.

The outboard motor coughed then started up,
pushing a rounded wave, while we watched
the dark and glittering sea. We left the harbour –
the boatshed on the wharf, the drop of shingle,
and soon our boat was climbing up a blue-green

hill of wave, which had a crest on top
that rippled, then slid down the other side,
my brothers grinning, my mother looking ill.
We let anchor down; rods were given out;
a bucket of dead mackerel thrown overboard.

And soon enough, just below the boat,
grey and serpentine, their lateral fins
held out: shark, the familiar nightmare shape –
one; another; more – ghostly nosings –
and just as soon my father caught one, thrashing

as he reeled it in. They weren't full-grown
or they were dog sharks, four feet long or so.
Robert caught one, smaller than the first,
Johnny followed suit and even I
got a bite, although the fisherman took over,

heaving it into the bottom of the boat
onto a black tarpaulin where it writhed
and rubbed away its silver and where our skipper,
a local man who lived behind the quay,
beat its brains out with a wooden rod,

a cudgel, like a policeman at a riot.
More and more were killed like that. My father
asked for it to stop but we only pulled up
anchor when the captain gave the word.
We set sail for home. A flock of seagulls

followed in our wake or risked their perchings
on the cabin roof. When we got back
to the quay and my thankful mother climbed
the jetty steps, my father paid the thirty pound
we owed but wouldn't shake the skipper's hand.

The Small Boy and the Mouse

When he closed his eyes and asked the question,
he saw an egg, a boiled egg, lodged
above his heart. The shell had been broken off,
with a teaspoon he supposed, it was pure curd white
and still warm. Inside – he could *see* inside –
there was a garden with rows of potatoes,
sweet peas in a tangle and a few tomatoes, red
and green ones, along with that funny sulphur smell
coming from split sacks. There was an enamel bathtub
in the garden with chipped edges, a brown puddle
staining around itself, and a few wet leaves.
He could see down the plughole, so the sun must have shone,
and he heard his father digging potatoes,
knocking off the soil, and his mother fetching the washing in
because the sky promised a shower. There was a hole
or rather a pipe under the tub where the water went
and down at the bottom was a mouse – its ribs were poking out,
its damp fur clung together. The mouse was holding
a black-and-white photograph of a boy
who might have been three or four years old;
the boy was playing with boxes, or were they saucepans
from the kitchen? – he was leaning forward and slightly blurred.
And what was strange about the picture,
apart from being held by a mouse who sat on his haunches
and gripped it in his forepaws, was that the space
around the boy, the paleness around him, expanded,
got very bright and engulfed the mouse, the bathtub,
the garden and the egg with its shell cracked off.
After that there was nothing, apart from the dark
inside the boy's head and a kind of quiet
he'd never had before. He opened his eyes. All the furniture
looked strange, as if someone had rearranged it.

II.

Still Life with Geranium

Nothing intervenes
except this mild
October sun
stepping down
on young geranium leaves
and apples on a plate,
each crescent light
a picture of the moon.
The armchair
takes my weight,
then takes away
my thought. The quiet
inside myself
is of a room inside a room.

Place

You're in a room
    with one high window

your stepladder doesn't reach.
    It's better

if you close your eyes
    but when you do

it's like sitting in an aviary.
    You can talk

of course, through the wall;
    you can knock knock knock

with a metal cup;
    you can sit and wait.

You screw up your eyes,
    fold a square of paper,

then let it go.
    Suddenly you're outside

looking in
    but through a fisheye lens:

all the walls are curved
    like the inside of a flower.

Blaen-y-Ddol

A farm boy sitting on a step takes off
his boots so the sun can warm his feet.
He's about the age when he can start a beard.
The sunlight in his eyes turns the alders
at the farmyard edge into barely moving patterns,
black-toothed against the fields. Midges crowd
the air – they twinkle almost in the sun
and make a sky of shavings. Some float on
like floating bits of straw, some go up-a-bit
down-a-bit, some make agitated columns.
The boy's damp socks stiffen as they dry
and when he stands he's taller than you think.
He ties his laces, then walks across a field.
You stop to watch him go. The midges catch
the light and make a thousand thousand tunnels:
the Tunnel of Love, the Tunnel of Lost-and-Found,
the Tunnel of All the Things you Mean to Keep.

Thought-path

I made a round of stones,
uneven stones,
        so I could walk

the needles in a circling
path of thought.
        Pine trees, rough as broken

masonry, leant up
among the shadows.
        I was like someone who goes

into a shop, lifts down a vase
or a statuette of Pan,
        then puts it back. I said out loud,

'Pine cones' – I bent my neck
to look: pine logs waiting
        for winter fires, holly oaks

and rock roses with all their
petals gone. A bird
        seemed to shake a rattle

for me to keep in step, while
another sang the same
        upward-sliding note. I was just

about to stop when a voice
(not my voice in my throat)
        said softly *please... please...*

Shipwright

You have to go outside and find a nut
that's been hidden under a leaf, a walnut
with drill holes where the grubs have wheedled in.

Break it open – everything inside
is blackened and shrivelled up. Flick away
the grubs, pale and liverish, then use

the better half, the half without the dark
and grainy spots. Knock the empty shell
against a stone, find a hawthorn twig

and a fingernail of bark and raise the fragile
riggings and the mast. Hoist a sail
made of a dying maple leaf or oak,

a little sail, then climb aboard and watch
the harbour as it folds away – the seafront
and the bright marina, the castle on the hill.

Bathymetry

His heart was made of greenhouse glass
leant up, pane on pane, and some of it cracked
with crumbling putty and paint-flakes

round the edge. Sunlight touched a patch
of condensation that rocked between the glass.
He knew the water was dead,

so it must have been the sun
that woke the strange green seagrass
waving with the current's pull and drag.

He noticed particles of grit suspended,
erythrocytes and leukocytes,
water-boatmen rowing across a brown

and choppy sea; but if there were oysters
among the mangrove roots,
they must have been very small indeed.

Colloquium

A bird came to a pine tree, perched on
branches grey and half-lit, waited
while the sea brightened and the hills shone.

The bird herself was grey, except for a flare
of white she meant to hide. She stopped
and changed her profile, then flew not far

to another tree inside the grove's silence.
She made a dove-like fussing while
the pine-tops greened. Some disturbance

in the branches brought another like the first,
with the same wine-bottle neck.
She made no music, but when she perched

a little further off, as she did on another
branch, there was the same brightness
under her wing. Another bird came, another

and yet another – they paused, divided perhaps
between five or so, six or so, pine trees.
And there they stayed. No time elapsed,
no wind came quickly across the marram grass.

Rangiatea

The sea was grey but the island was missing.
Irregular in the half-haze, like the haunches
of a dog, the island was battleship grey
and heading south. The dead had stopped
before their journey across the waves.

A cormorant, standing on a rock,
looked like the phoenix on a family crest,
terns snatched fish from the skipping sea,
groups of seagulls gathered along its shore
and light touched pebbles in the muffling bays.

The sun rose on gorse bushes and birds,
it rose on broken shells and on the sea
where the clouds had shone, it rose
above wooded peaks, making curtained
shadows on the flanks of hills, it rose

and it set, turning the trees bright red.
At night, a full moon created an isle of frost
and a phosphorescent sea, then it became
a shape of night in the centre of night
with just a few stars hung above it.

No boats made the journey, no fishermen
with nets, no guns, harpoons, no invaders
or men with measuring sticks. Every day
was like the last: curlews fretted among
the tides, crabs lived quietly under stones,

fish were moving patterns in the sea.
Beyond the northern ridge, a white whale sang.
It was 'The place out there', *Rangiatea*
as the Maori say, somewhere you could stay
and find the peace you wanted; somewhere

you could watch the blue deepening
and deepening, hear the gulls cry
and the breakers breaking: somewhere
you could sit and think the whole thing over.
But now the island was missing.

*

No one remembered the island, except a man,
a bachelor who looked after his mother
till she died. He often dreamt of it –
curving bays and birds, four miles out
and hidden, half-hidden in the cloud.

He couldn't decide if the island was real
or just the interval between sleeping
and waking, known only from the corner
of your eye – a star you couldn't see head-on,
a seal above the rolling waves and watching.

He thought he remembered the journey out,
his mother worried by the boat, his father
impatient to arrive, but the memory
was blurred like a story he'd been told
or just another beach he went to as a child.

Had they let him play there on his own? –
the tiny break of shells under his sandalled feet,
the quiet stretching so far he heard a wave
turning out at sea? There were seagulls
on the mirrored sand, his mother asking for him

but not recognising him, her frightened look
whenever he turned her over to rub her back,
the struggle with her nightdress, her grip
so tight he had to peel away her hand,
how ridged and reddened her skin was

from where the sheets had gathered up.
The nurse came twice a day, once to put her
in her chair and once to lift her out,
all the other visitors had stopped.
He'd grown tired of sympathetic words.

But the day she died, everything rang out –
quietly, quietly – with a kind of sense,
a pattern he could touch. He thought
the answer (if there was one) must be
simple, like looking slightly to the left.

*

There were so many beautiful men that summer,
lying on the seafront, their backs prickled
by dead grass, their white skin flushed.
They swam or slept. Their knotted arms
were like ropes thrown into clear water.

And there were many beautiful women too,
sitting on the rocks, dabbling their fingers
in the icy pools, watching the water-boatmen
and rubbing cream on their sunburnt breasts.
Their sea-wet hair clung to their necks.

The town behind them had clapboard houses
and a church with a corrugated roof.
It looked like England: gravestones and lawns,
flowerbeds and creosoted fences.
The shops sold hand-woven rugs

and bath towels with seahorse designs.
There were boating lakes and running tracks,
places set aside with hand-bars and benches,
picnic spots, designated views with plaques
that told you the meaning of things

and the meaning of names – place names,
bird names, the different kinds of rushes
or shell creatures. All the narrow roads
ran right up to the farms, which had spacious
verandas and netted windows open all year.

Everyone had a garden, a paddling pool
or a basketball hoop fixed above the garage door.
And when it was fine or when a breeze
fluttered the washing, men in golf caps
painted their boats on the shingled strand.

Couples sat outside until the sunlight failed
and the sea darkened and the streets
were peppered with neon. Groups of friends
laughed and talked as they wandered home,
the white of their shirts flaring in the dark.

*

He didn't change his life. He bought a dog,
had the house repainted, fixed the rattling
panes and spent more time working
in the garden or facing out to sea.
He drank little or none at all, didn't smoke,

kept regular hours, read in the evening –
periodicals mostly, about carpentry or shrubs –
and sometimes sat for hours in the dark.
He felt a change of heart, yes, some shifting
but he couldn't explain it, even to himself.

He'd sit and listen to the surf or a handful
of rain thrown like grit against the glass –
the horizon stretched across the window,
grey clouds becoming other greys –
or he'd take the dog out and let her run

while he passed the time with neighbours –
the woman from the shop, the man
with blue tattoos who fixed his boat.
Nothing came of it. He'd call the dog
and walk her back to the empty house –

the thud...thud...of the returning tide
like distant cannon. A seagull shrieked
above the roof, the wind answered
by pushing on a pane, and later when
he listened to his clocks, the full moon rose

making a deeper night and a phantom day.
Sometimes he'd fall asleep and dream
about the island once again – seaweed
floating like dishevelled hair, the ocean
throwing ropes of falling water

up against the stars – but when he woke,
still sitting in his chair, all that lingered
was the name – *Rangiatea, Rangiatea* –
while beyond the house, the muffled sound
of waves was like the breathing dead.

Sierra Aitana

This housefly buzzing
    in frenzied circles;
this lizard, fast across
    a stone; this injured
forager ant half-mad
    with pain; this bird
among the branches
    constantly glancing up
like a foreigner dining alone
    in a strange hotel;
and me sitting in the sun –
    a narrow text of rancour
running through my heart.

Pine Branch

Cézanne would have understood the problem
of a pine branch, its relation to the sky
in the early morning with just a sickle moon
and the sun not yet up among the rocks.

He would have felt its half-gesture – arm
outstretched in something less than beckoning,
pine cones open, flowering or shut.
He would have made it the subject of one of his

'experiments', felt, with the tip of his brush,
the branch's articulation – slender, more
slender – needles curling back, the thinnest
twig diamonding the blue or ramifying into it.

Letters on Cézanne

Rilke said when he went to the Salon d'Automne
with Mathilde Vollmoeller to see the Cézannes
or perhaps it was Mathilde who said it and Rilke
wrote about it in one of those letters to his wife,
letters describing days of rain and going every day
to see the Cézannes, that the colour of his paintings,
each colour knowing every other colour in a
perpetual dialogue and exchange, that the colours
blended in the air around them, mixed into a neutral
grey, an atmosphere of equipoise, almost velvetlike –
the black and white only defining the limits of his
wide-open palette. It should be the same with us:
the Yes balancing out the No, Joy calming Despair
without cancellation: a day of sun and a day of rain.

The Theory of Touch

One theory was that the sense of handling – each apple
cupped in his palm and every colour weighed
so it became the thing itself – the tabletop, the pear –
one theory was that this caressing light across a wall,
this reaching out to feel each surface, sprung from phobia:
at school a boy had pushed him down the stairs
so even as an old man his son would have to say
'You'll forgive me father if I take your arm.'

Even in his final year when Émile Bernard reached to help him
on uneven ground, Cézanne cried out and shook him off.
I'm sated with touch. Last night I touched your face,
your arms, your chest as if touching would prove
some use against the coming loss; as if I'd keep you
like he kept those – how many? – apples on a box.

Putting Away Pictures

When a painting lost its lustre,
it improved, Braque said,
if you put it in the sun
to warm the madder browns
and umbers. People laughed at that.
But paintings do improve
if you put them in a drawer
or like reprimanded
children, turn them to face the wall.
No one rearranges
the forms, adjusts the faulty profile
of a tree, the figure
out of kilter with the ground;
no one modulates
the colour key, takes it down
a pitch or two: shadows
and a wall are all that's needed
to make amends.
The same could be said of you.

Lady with a Chaffinch

The heart in infrared and ultraviolet shows
no underdrawing: chromatography

confirms the attribution is correct.
The walnut panel is of the requisite age.

The armoured soldiers on the hill, the greenwood
by the cliff, the chaffinch the lady holds

as she turns towards your gaze, nothing
in the underpainting suggests

its provenance is in any way suspect.
Sometimes the attribution is correct.

Hill Town

At the outposts of this little town people tell us they see sights
– strange lights and apparitions – but no one can say if they're
imagining it or if it's true. Some say prayers, others value
wearing particular kinds of clothing. The town is on a hill
and should have views but the sea mist blocks them off.
There's no main road to speak of but the major roads criss-
cross avenues lined with lemon trees and pears. There are
many shops, as you would expect – ice cream parlours, small
restaurants selling the local mackerel dish, a bank with an
imposing portico of columns. The streets are so narrow people
can talk from their bedroom window to their neighbour across
the street; they can pass across a meal or newspaper. It's not
completely clear what work these people do but they all look
busy and are nicely dressed. Coach parties are organised each
year to go out to the frontiers, but we can't tell from our
reports who believes in anything they're told, who in nothing
and who looks beyond existence and non-existence to something
in between.

Ornithology

In that other world, woodpigeons were considered rare and very beautiful. All the other birds were brown or Spanish black, so at the sound of cooing, children were allowed to put away their books and run into the playground, just in case. Bankers, in the midst of board meetings, pressed their faces to the glass. Once a mating pair came to Central Park. They had to keep the crowds in check while worried ornithologists begged the public not to use a flash. Filmcrews were despatched. Many amateur photographers arrived. The chicks were remembered in the press and given honorific names. Painters had them flapping in a tree or wading through the grass, but poets were advised not to labour their troubled song with iridescence or the colour of a breast.

Mariner

He set himself the task of finding perfect neutral without exaggeration or colouring-in, a kind of mildness like the taste of heated milk. He thought of camomile and cotton buds, dock leaves rubbed against your shin, but there were ghosts inside his body – winding sheets and chainmail, old linen, old flags, pouches of lavender – and if he thought in one way everything went orange, and if he thought another, grey. He wasn't sure if the closed-in feeling inside his chest was cockleshell or devil's toenail. (He couldn't prise it open with a knife or crack it open like a nut.) It seemed to him to do with boiler rooms and battleships – a man running down flight after flight of metal steps until he reached a smoke-filled engine room where a huddled group of sailors hunched across a grubby pack of cards.

The Marvellous Toy

He opened the marvellous toy on the kitchen floor. It didn't need a plug. It might have been a fan belt or clothes pegs pegged together in a round. It hovered just above the linoleum, twitched slightly, then the lights came on. It spun. And as it spun the colours changed like traffic lights or the many coloured bulbs above the waltzers. Music started – pop music mostly in little snatches – words, sentences in different voices, a hubbub, an auditorium of sound. Then it was a figure of eight, a reef knot, the calyx of a lotus flower, a spiral shell, a Broadway boogie-woogie. Nothing could stop it. Even when his mother told him to turn it off, he could still hear it pulsating in its box.

At the Station

Two men in a crowd alighting at Euston.
One is blond and wears a polo shirt
with the collar turned up and 22 stencilled
on the back, the other has close-cropped hair.
They could be members of a rowing crew.

The blond one slips his ticket into the pocket
of the other's jeans, puts his arm around him
and draws him slightly closer – a gesture
so unforced they might have been at home.
They move across the crowded concourse

heading for the tube, where I follow
down the escalator to the waiting train.
I watch them steady themselves
in the tunnel's rush, eyes cast down, shoulders
knocking slightly as their bodies sway.

They seem so easy, smiling into themselves,
letting their bare arms touch. They get off
at a station far away, buy oranges and milk,
then walk quietly to their flat, where
without hurry, they take off all their clothes.

One wraps his arms around the other
from behind. He can feel his belly's breath
against his back. They stay like this
for quite some time, like figures made of clay
still warm from the hand that fashioned them.

Umbrian Summer

Even though the wind
was warm and we slept
with the window open,

next day
there were beech leaves
on the swimming pool –

chrome yellow
on a zone of blue,
like something Japanese.

The sun
had seemed to shine
through lemonade –

it lingered
on the other hill and made
the shadows gentler.

Night fell slowly
on the drive.
The full moon drifted

high above a ridge,
half-covered
in a shawl of cloud –

she seemed so
pale and cold,
pronouncing Oṃ and Autumn.

The Man

The man was sitting by his kitchen window.
Outside, the trees were full of nervous birds,
nodding their heads or flicking up their tails
in gestures of defiance. A pheasant walked
along a hedge, his copper coat restrained,
even the sun held back behind the trees.
The man was watching ladybirds climb up
the windowpane: so many on the walls,
so many huddled near the lights! They fell
down on their backs as if they'd taken ether.

The house stood in the corner of a field
with woodpigeons, always woodpigeons, in twos
or squadrons in the trees; and a robin singing
from a post, his song as bright as teaspoons.
The sun rose in pale and broken stripes,
then set in a perfect orange ball. Nothing
happened inside the house. The man took off
his glasses when he slept, drank two strong cups
of coffee every day and walked around
the garden with his scarf around his neck.

He wanted signs of life: the sound of someone
closing a drawer or slipping on a jacket;
but no one pressed the gravel drive or opened
the kitchen door. A patch of sunlight swivelled
round the room, brightening the kettle's spout.
The man lay down and wrote inspiring things
on little scraps of card. He thought he heard
a hare snuffling in the grass, an owl
hooting at the night. But then the taps
ran dry and the blue pilot light went out.

The Squirrel Sutra

Walking to the water trough
I stopped to see a squirrel stop,
a red squirrel drinking at the tap.

Hearing me it climbed the first
thin branches of a pine, then looked
to see if I was any kind of threat.

And as I stood, a blackcap settled
on a branch, then hummingbird-like
seemed to stop midair while

the Yellow King with his horde
of hungry ghosts, the White King
surrounded by celestial musicians,

the Red King with his entourage
of kumbhāṇḍas and fever spirits,
and the Green King took their stand.

Something Happened

Something happened in the dark,
the dark of your closed eyes,
early after the moon had set
behind the blackened pines.

Your body ached; your head was bowed
but not towards his face.
A heron flew up from your sleep
to find a better place.

It was cold and you were tired.
Half-dreams came and went
while you made your way below
to where the heart relents.

Lullaby

Your eyes are tired now, they're tired.
Put him away and go to sleep:
the plaster lion in the garden,
lichen clinging to his mane,
with furious eyes and curving teeth –
let his cold ambition quieten.

Your eyes are tired now, they're tired.
Put them away and go to sleep:
the playhouse and the plastic dishes,
shuttered window, open door;
put your love away, its wishes –
the man and all you loved him for.

Your eyes are tired now, they're tired.
Put everything away and sleep:
the lion's claws, the Wendy house,
applause from those around you – weep
for what you meant to do and will.
Close your eyes and sleep.

Homecoming

If I had to think of a place,
    I'd think of those cold shallows
        where the dogs drank
and I threw a stick
and everything was patterned with sycamore.
    I'd think of myself as a child
        falling asleep
in the back of the Austin Princess.

I'd think of our being together
        as a small thing –
picking up a windfall
    or pouring a tumbler-full of water –
        the moment, extended,
when an engine stops and time folds away.

You were blurred,
        as though through chlorine –
your rose-body wavered,
    breaking up,
        your limbs made ripples
when I spoke.

    We were there together.
And it might have been
    at the top of the garden
near the hole-in-the-hedge,
        or it might have been anywhere
between traffic noise,
    in the Sunday silence of the high street.

The Master

The wind dies in the larches —a gust takes them,
        rocks them,

     then slows everything to a standstill:
         grandma holding the boys,
your father by the tool shed,
     Stephen standing by the dodgems
        waiting for you to speak.

You have to find the one who's always outside,
        always stepping down,
   but you only have pictures
     to go on,
        pictures covered with tracing paper.

You wish you were standing on the Mount.
        You wish it had snowed
  and you were taking the dogs out –
     Ajax scenting a rabbit,
        your breath making plumes.

But you can't imagine it,
   skirting the church
     where your parents walked
        under an avenue of cricket bats.

You can see the path
     past the graveyard where your grandmother
        wouldn't have a stone,
   you can see St Nicholas' and St John's –
     the edge of your roof,

     the whole of Brook End Drive –
but you can't see him:
     the Master of Minnows and Crayfish.

Reading Elizabeth Jennings

This is a good model; words that hold
across the page and can say
'rose' or 'river' seriously,
without disdain,

can take as subject frost or rain,
the taste of tea. My thoughts
(she helps me say it now) break in
and spoil it all:

the body that might fall
around itself, the breath finding
an old zinc bucket to rock itself in
and the lotus opening.

Visitation

Strange that you should come
like that, without any form at all,
carrying no symbolic implements,
without smile or frown
or any commotion,
as if you had been there all the time,
like a pair of gloves left in a pocket.

As if I had been looking *that* way,
into the wide blue yonder, and you were
beside me, enduring my hard luck stories
with infinite patience. Not even waiting –
the tree outside my window
doesn't wait, nor the ocean-wedge
with its new, precise horizon – just there
like the shadow of a church

or a quiet brother.
And how I saw you, in the mess of things,
was as a slant of grey,
the perfect grey of house dust,
an absolute neutral, with no weaving,
no shimmer of cobalt
and light-years away from Byzantium.

Grey. And I want to add, like light,
as if a skylight opened in my skull,
and into the darkness fell
a diagonal of pure Bodmin Moor.
But even that's too bright,
too world-we're-busy-in.
Call it 'dust' then, or the bloom
of leaf-smoke from an autumn fire.

III. STEPHEN

Two Boys

Two boys once walked across an iron bridge,
one taller than the other. They didn't speak
or catch each other's eye. The brook they crossed

was finger-deep and running over pebbles,
it sounded like someone filling in a form,
writing all the answers with a pencil.

Cattle might have watched them as they hugged
the field's perimeter, the barbed-wire fence
and sycamores (this was before the age

of shaving, before the age of sex). No one
knew they knew each other, saw each other,
walked to Fletcher's Hole beside the brook.

It didn't matter now. It was long ago –
Trippers and Westmacott's, the Post Office,
The Golden Cross, the walk up Crockett's Lane.

History

When war was certain, my grandmother buried
the best crockery behind the pigsty,
although family legend has it that by armistice
she'd forgotten where. Either way,
if you dug between the garage and the hedge,
you found broken dinner plates, smashed-up
pudding bowls, apostle spoons and bed warmers.
The sty came down the year my grandma died.
It left a gap that soon filled up with lorry tyres
and scrap – a twin-tub lying on its side.
We'd meet and go there after school. I'd slip
between the leaning planks and snag my coat,
he'd follow me in with something like a smile.
We knelt and touched but hardly ever spoke.

The Cutting

The cutting at the end of Crockett's Lane
had a meadow on either side, a brow
fringed with blackthorn and a few sheep grazing
in sodden fields below. It carried steam trains
up to Lapworth, before the Beeching Axe
cut the branch lines down; now it was
a brambled 'V' overrun with elderflowers
and buddleia. We'd go there blackberrying,
filling colanders and plastic tubs –
the cutting was a good walk from the house,
almost far enough to tire the dogs.
I remember children on the embankment
carrying Union Jacks – up against
the sky like little soldiers. They came from all
the local schools because we'd heard the Queen
would visit Henley in the royal train.
But that can't be right: that line came up
before I was even born and only dad
remembered steam trains huffing up and down it.
I took Stephen there one summer; we kicked up
dandelions and it was hot; we got those
sticky burrs stuck to our shorts and socks.
We were looking for somewhere we'd be safe
and out of sight, a cleft beside a pond,
and as we walked two pigeons clattered out.
We waded nettles that reached up to our chest.
I managed to lift his shirt and touch his side,
but he was scared and so was I. And anyway
the train didn't stop; we just stood there
on the platform while she thundered past.

The Brook

Standing on a bridge in the beginnings
of snow, taking the measure of it –
the water's reach, trees reflected,
the careening white of gulls,

I was trying to hold, trying
to keep it all – the river's elbowing,
the valley's palm. He was standing
on a bridge and couldn't speak –

water racing over pebbles
and half-bricks, a sound like muted
ovation, like an audience constantly
rising to its feet. I was looking

to where the silted leaves might show
a trout or stickleback, a sluggish
weight of water. He was waiting
by the dam beside the brook.

The Dam

When we came to our usual stopping place,
where the brook ran over a flight of steps,
the last remains of an ancient, blue-brick dam
that long before my time had turned the current
toward a millwheel, we waited at the edge
and kept a look-out. Either side the brook –
the side we stood on and the further bank
where trees ran right up to the road – the walls
of the dam, or what was left of them,
were wide enough to sit on. The current turned
an elbow at that point and in the crook
white pebbles shone like an island below
the leaning trees – you could get across
with your trousers rolled, but it was deep
a little further off and ran in eddies
and whirlpools. Stephen walked a step or two
ahead while I listened beyond our footfalls
and the early evening traffic in case someone
was walking nearby, someone my parents
would've known and I should say hello to
(I never took the dogs; I couldn't bear
for them to watch). We found a place to hide,
made private with ivy belts and stingers,
then we spread our coats out on the ground.

Dogs

I watched his father's garage from where I stood
on the old embankment: no sign of him –
the green door closed, the tidy garden empty.
I would have waited longer but the dogs
jumped up and whined and wouldn't let me stay.
The cutting curved behind the backs of council houses –
garden sheds and wire fences marked
each garden's end above the brambly bank.
The dogs ran on to chase the scent of other dogs.
I walked along behind with just one thought.

Fields stretched away towards the scout hut
and the line to Stratford still in use – the cutting
used to join it further on coming in from Lapworth
but now gave way to clouds and farmers' crops.
A train was pulling into Henley and even
from this distance I could see people getting up,
reaching down a bag or folding up a newspaper.
The dogs, scenting a change of heart, were keen
to stop – we'd not gone far, just far enough
for them to 'do their business' as my mother said.

I'd been stretching out the time with hope
that when I got back to Johnson Place – the path
up to the embankment where I'd stood before –
I'd see him in the garage with his moped,
oiling the brakes, maybe mending a puncture
with his bike tipped up on its handlebars.
But by the time I got there, rain had started tapping
on my anorak, making the dogs' ears twitch.
No sign. I walked as slowly as I could
to the path that led beside his father's garage.

The Garden

After we did it under the hedge
where two hawthorns met
near the cooking-apple tree
and the wreck of the Austin Princess,
I ran down the April garden

past my father's potatoes drills.
I knew it was wrong. I ran.
And under cherry blossom
between the tomato greenhouse
and another pile of scrap

I nearly collided with my mum
coming from the washing line,
her basket full of sunny sheets
and brothers' shirts, her arms
freckled with (how I saw it) love.

That night I prayed to Jesus.
He was standing on a hill
surrounded by animals – two lambs,
a goat, a flock of sparrows.
I prayed no one would ever know.

Canaries

His father's garden shed had a bitumen roof,
a single window and a bolted door;
but when I pushed it open (he must have stood behind)

the shock was Easter yellow
and racketing in the overheated space.
Beyond the floor-to-ceiling chicken wire,

budgerigars like multi-coloured child-size owls
fluttered from perch to perch and there were cuttlefish
at different heights for them to do their beaks on.

He must have stood behind or waited outside.
I must have asked to see them. But was it when
we took the school bus home from Wootton Wawen

or later when I lied about his homework?
I don't know how I stood among the songs.

Blazon

If I can't remember the colour of your eyes
(I'll say that they were green) or the timbre
of your voice; if I can't recall the contour
of your chest (which was hairless skin and bone);

if you never told me what you thought
about school or Mr Callaghan, The Winter
of Discontent; if I can't decide whether
the last time was stood in front of your back door

or when you followed me up Tanworth Lane
that time I had a weekend gardening job;
if I can't remember you passing me in the street
or me dawdling – you coming up behind

and saying quietly, quickly, where you'd be –
if I can't remember that, Stephen
(your arms down by your sides and whiplash-thin),
then let me fold you in these white sheets.

The Mop

The Mop came once a year and blocked the High Street.
The route past Station Road became a web
of cables, spools and drums, with wires snaking
across the road or slung from stall to stall.
Gypsies in high-sided lorries with mongrels
on their laps and boys with sullen eyes
spent most of the day erecting the ghost train
and the coconut shy. Goldfish hung
in plastic bags between the flashing lights –
they'd swell up then go back to normal size.

By evening, ropes of coloured lights hung
between the limes. *Sylvester* filled the air
along with candyfloss and diesel fumes;
cars flung you back and forth and waltzers
spun you round while you held the bar
and screamed – a man would walk the rising-falling
floor like he was striding across the sea,
although he nearly always chose the girls.
Yellow plastic ducks swam together
in a revolving circle backed by mirror glass,

each one had a wire hoop under its bill
so if you managed to hook one out a gypsy
would read the number felt-tipped on the base,
then pass across a pair of Spanish dancers
or a plaster-of-Paris fish – flat and white
and chalky from behind. I never played
the one-armed bandits, but I liked the fruit –
spinning lemons, strawberries and pears,
the handle-pull, the regurgitated money.
Stephen was standing with a group of friends

just inside the tent. I kept my eyes
averted although something must have ached;
he turned away but didn't join the taunts.
That must have been the year I said I'd take
my Nana to the Mop, but when Penny came
or Pauline, I forgot and she sat all evening
waiting in the house. I think I see him
standing by the dodgem steps, hands
inside his pockets, his face flashing amber,
red and green. Girls were getting off,

feeling wobbly and having to sit down
while a man would run across to help each time
too many cars collided. The Mop had gone
by morning, the streets were quiet again and dull,
they'd even swept and cleared away the litter.
It was around the start of autumn, the air
had that sudden softness, leaves were turning –
he'd been waiting to do something with his life
when someone screamed as a woman we both knew
turned right and knocked him off his bike.

Wild Bees

The railway bridge across the A45
just beyond the High Street was demolished
when I was ten or so – workmen in hardhats
with acetylene torches cut the iron trusses

into slabs and blocked the weekday traffic.
I used to walk across it and look down
at cars coming in and out of Henley –
my father's lorry, a coach returning home.

The path to Lodder's field was further on:
the dogs squeezed through a stile when I let them.
We'd go there on our own, Stephen and me,
down a steep and weedy slope this side

of an old footbridge so hidden in the ground
you didn't know you were walking on a bridge.
Usually we'd hide inside the arch
that once had spanned a millstream, long dried up,

strewn with bags and opened tins of dog food
where a tramp was said to sleep, but this time
we pushed along the ditch to find a hideout
near the road – a den we only went to once,

where I'd tried the words 'I love you', then kissed
his tight shut mouth. We must have disturbed a nest
of wild bees and made them mad. I ran away
with bees tangled, fizzing in my hair.

He watched me go. That was before they turned
Beaudesert Park into expensive flats;
before Haven Pastures became a golf club;
before someone burnt the scout hut down.

Caravan

I was washing up in a narrow kitchenette
with the wind blowing at the door
and everything small like they have in caravans.
Beyond the window, fields and dripping bracken
fell away to where the river was in spate.
I was looking at a bank of cowslips.

Suddenly there you were behind and slightly
to my right. I could almost hear you breathe,
your weight perhaps shifting from foot to foot.
I was so surprised I said 'Stephen?'
out loud into the silence: you behind me
like a farm cat rubbing on my calf.

You seemed to wait a moment as if you had
a question. Outside, a tractor laboured up
a hill – engine noise trailing off,
then hanging on after the tractor disappeared.
Something gave, not a sigh exactly,
a shrug almost, before you turned away.

Trenches

It must have been after the final No,
I can't make sense of it otherwise,
how I felt, the way he pulled his moped round –
he was near the path that led up the embankment
and even from so far away, something

was agreed. I pedalled as fast as I could
beyond a row of houses set back from the road –
Mr Wilson's house where I'd been ashamed,
when I was invited round, to take off my shoes.
Stephen must have overtook and gone ahead

but when I got to The Bird in Hand,
he came around behind and slowed right down.
No one was about. It was a Sunday morning.
I don't know how I knew that to my right –
after we stopped and he pulled his moped

on its stand and flipped his helmet off,
my bike lying on its side – the ground fell away
to a farmer's ditch, a bank we skidded down,
deep enough to be hidden from the road.
We did whatever it was we did

then climbed back up – Stephen pulling on
his gauntlets while I trembled with the bike
and rode to my gardening job where
the potato trenches I dug were so out of true
the owner said I must have been in love.

Fireworks

And now I almost see you after school
in the early evening, your presence stepping
softly through the hedge, a skip of shadow
becoming your familiar-unfamiliar ghost.
You wait beside the cooking-apple tree
then cut across the playing field to where
the intervening years have added lightness
as you make your way along my father's coaches
hoisted up on bricks, the plum my grandma
sat beside to watch the autumn picking,
the walnut and the rockery. You duck
inside the den behind the old green lorry
(I've been waiting all this time to find out
what it was you felt) but when I turn to ask
you're back under the shade of silver birches.
This time we'll watch the fireworks go up.
I'll step behind the hedge and join you watching
in the dark – sparklers and hotdogs,
the catherine wheel, the rockets' spew of gold –
and first thing in the morning we'll go out
to find the blackened sticks and canisters.

The Name

I don't remember seeing you in the snow
by the playing field, below the silver birches.

I don't remember autumn or when we met,
whether or not your skin was warm, what kind

of clothes you wore, what you thought about
the first Apollo landing. There were summers

of course, eight of them, and spring, the hedges
coming back and flowering; but I don't

remember the name I called you on the bus,
the one you chased and hit me for while I stood

on the Butlers' lawn, or what you looked like
that evening at the Mop. I remember you

climbing up the kitchen stairs, naked
on your hands and knees, and me following.

Newspapers

My father kept the baled-up newspapers
inside the old green lorry. They mouldered
in the summer heat – the page three girl,
Snoopy at the back of the *Daily Mail*,
UFOs and the mask of Tutankhamun.
He kept them for the scouts, along with gold
and silver bottle tops. The lorry was near
the hedge where I lost my mother's breadknife.

My brothers jumped off the lorry roof
onto bales of hay, Robert going first,
but when it came to my turn I hit my jaw
against my knee and ran down the garden crying.
Next door's garden was overgrown with weeds.
When the neighbour died, my father said,
he left instructions which compost heap
his body should be left on. We went there once.

Raspberries and redcurrants were tangled up
in briars and there were runner beans
choked with nettles still growing on their sticks.
Stephen managed to force the back door open.
We climbed the narrow buckled stair that led
up to a box room lined with newspapers
leftover from where the underlay had been.
A single window overlooked the ruined garden.

It felt like everyone could see, so he climbed
up through the attic hatch until his legs
disappeared into the dark. That must have been
a year before he was killed at the intersection
between Beaudesert Lane and the High Street,
his body lying under a blanket in the road,
the ambulance stopping the traffic and me walking
to school, the morning of my art exam.

A Few Fields

He had a landscape in his head: neat fields
with sheep, stopping and chewing, then moving on,
measuring the distance between the embankment
pocked with rabbit holes, the abandoned house
and railway bridge. And if it was a map
inside his head instead of moving pictures,
he could walk his fingers from bridge to bridge, imagine
nettles and the smell of wild garlic.

Each bridge would tell a different story: a crayfish
hidden inside a plastic shoe; the place
the dog jumped in and barked and bit the water;
The Black Swan's lawn. He'd walk his fingers down
the bridal path where they'd hid together,
then back along the brook towards St John's
and the picture hanging in the nave
of Christ, reproachful, carrying the cross.

The First Time

I wanted this to be the first time, back
to Lodder's field beside the bending brook,

the shingled side, overhanging trees
that seemed to be so high, the blue-brick wall

I lay on in the sun – the dogs standing
ankle-deep and impatient – an iron bridge

I looked down from and watched the light
folding and unfolding rooms of water.

I wanted this to be the place I learnt
how warm your skin could be, even in winter.

The Usual Things

I should say time didn't hurt you or turn you grey,
make you stoop or gasp when you stood up,
grow beer-bellied, fat and idle by the television –
your youth worn out in marriage or inconsequence.

I should say you were saved from the usual shocks,
the simple disappointments, the standard cost
of error which anyway would take away your life:
Hansel never grew up; the crumb road lost.

I should say you were my love, but you were not.
You stand in twilight on your father's lawn
(no blackbird sings in a small-minded English town)
and when I try to touch you, you push me off.

Snow

I want to imagine you
into this room

this morning.
I want to see you

listen to the sound
(can you hear it?)

of snow thawing,
falling, sliding

down the roof tiles –
there, and there again

like billiard balls
rolling across the baize

or blinds drawn down,
weight on white

weight, slowly,
heavily to the ground.

Retrospect

In my story, you walked to school that day,
left the moped in the garage with your
gauntlets on the seat, caught up with me,
suggested we should meet back at your house,
your brother still at work. I tell myself
we carry on from there, off and on
until I move away. Now you're twenty-five
and have learnt the art of smiling. We talk
about that time you waited in the bath
next to your parents' kitchen after school.
But the story won't make sense, the facts
you left too small to be given consequence.
I can't put explanations in your mouth.
You just stand there in the kitchen doorway,
pencil-slim and pale and carrying a helmet.